# AFRICAN HISTORY

## FOR BEGINNERS

### Part 1: African Dawn — A Diasporan View

**WRITERS AND READERS PUBLISHING, INC.**
P.O. Box 461, Village Station
New York, NY 10014

Writers and Readers Limited
9 Cynthia Street
London N1 9JF
England

•

A Writers and Readers Documentary Comic Book Copyright © 1994

ISBN # 0-86316-144-8
2 3 4 5 6 7 8 9 0

Manufactured in the United States of America

Beginners Documentary Comic Books are published by Writers and Readers
Publishing Inc. Its trademark, consisting of the words "For Beginners, Writers
and Readers Documentary Comic Books" and the Writers and Readers logo, is
registered in the U.S. Patent and Trademark Office and in other countries.

# AFRICAN HISTORY
## For Beginners
### Part 1: African Dawn – A Diasporan View

To the Children of Africa

Written by **Herb Boyd**

> — *To Elza and the Katherines*

Illustrated & designed by **Shey Wolvek-Pfister**

> — *To the memory of Lillian, my mother,*
> *and to Sirka, my daughter and life spirit.*

Drawings of the Griot and the
Leopard Woman Story by **Bernard Aquina Doctor**

# FIRST WORDS

Call me Olagun. I am a **griot,** a master of words and memory, a keeper of the flame and the history of my people who dwell in the rain forests and the deserts, and beyond the distant African plains and savannas. I descend from the immortal griot Mamadou Keita of **Mali** and trace my ancestry back to the first African dawn. Since those primordial days my family has been the village griots, the talking books, who have not forgotten their duty to keep "the keys to the twelve doors of Mali."

*Call me Olagun.*

Do not take lightly my words because they are recited and not written. What is said, a proverb of my people informs, lives the same eternity as that which is chiseled on a cave wall or scratched upon parchment. A talking book is no less valuable than one whose words are silent. To see history through the eyes of the Whites is nothing when you can hear it from the lips of a griot.

Remember, a written note of music from the kora is but an approximation of the actual sound.

Hear my words, for I am but a vessel, a conduit through which the past is revealed, our history etched on the wind. Listen then, **Children of Africa**, we have had a glorious past and it presages a promising future.

In my generation, the fifteenth in our lineage, the **Mandingo**, the **Bambara**, the **Fulani**, and the **Ashanti** are threatened by a storm gathering in the north. There is much coming and going here in my village of Belandougou near the Sankarani river, within an arrow's flight from the tomb of Sundiata, the greatest of the **Mali** kings.

Already there are murmurs of war and pestilence in the silk-cotton trees and the divination stones foretell of great sailing boats from the north bearing *jinns* and evil ghosts. The griots, knowing that *"all true learning should be a secret,"* have assembled from the four corners of the continent to make sure the past is secured from the invaders.

I, Olagun, the son of Omawale, because of my power to invoke the past and to predict the future, have been asked to speak. It is my task to open the first door, to speak of events since the dynasty of the **Almoravids** and the reign of **Tenkhamenin**.

But before the truth can be told of those days—and before it is time for us during this rainy season to feast upon the carcass of the boar—we must remember the first legends and myths, the secrets before the flood and regeneration, before our queen mothers gave us the privilege to play our songs on the balafons and talking drums.

We must return to the land beyond Lake Chad, before the time of pharaohs and pyramids, to the beginning of the talking book when the first word was a whisper.

It was told to me by my father, who was told
by his father's father and passed along from
the family of **Ogun** and **Shango** that the first
breath of humankind occurred in Africa.
Thus, my children, our oldest ancestors
stepped from the mist and darkness 40,000
harvests ago. These black ancestors ventured
from that "ancient Eden," setting out to
discover the land beyond the **Mountains of
the Moon**, beyond the vast savannas and veld
land especially to build major civilizations
here and all over the world.

> *It is more probable that our early progenitors lived on the African continent than elsewhere.*

I owe to a gift of prophecy a way of knowing how the first bones will offer hints of the dark past. How, in the coming days the prophets of your time, such as **Charles Darwin**, will write of man's descent. Listen, for this sage speaks a truth, a truth that has been a part of our legends and songs since the Word was given to us by the gods. It is from our issue that all others are traced. It is part of the same story that the archeologists, **L.S.B.** and **Mary Leakey** will tell in another future generation.

I can envision the moment when Mary Leakey stumbles upon that jawbone of a hominid at Olduvai Gorge and can see how she and her husband will then assemble the puzzle of fragments into a complete cranium.

The skull will talk to them as it does in our myths and legends.

In **Nupe,** you may have heard, a hunter in pursuit of a water buffalo tripped over a skull. . .

*"Ah! What do we have here? And how did you get in my path?"*

*Talking brought me here.*

Amazed at the skull's ability to speak, the hunter ran back to the village to tell of his encounter. The king, hearing of the hunter's tale, was curious to see and hear this talking skull.

The hunter led the king with his retinue of guests to the spot in the forest. The king approached the skull and asked ...

*How did you get here?*

But the skull was silent. After several inquiries the skull still refused to speak. Now the king was furious and ordered his soldiers to cut the hunter's head off on the spot.

Later, after the king and his party were gone, the skull spoke to the hunter:

*Well, my friend, how did you get here?*

The hunter replied:

*Talking brought me here.*

The skull of myth and proverb teaches us one lesson, while the bones the Leakeys and their team of anthropologists led by Kamoya Kimeu will find imparts another truth. These bones, like the talking skull, will give them a passage to the past and a lighted way into the deep mysteries of my people's history. But hush now and let me tell you what the talking bones told our diviners centuries before the scientists of your day came with their microscopes and telescopes.

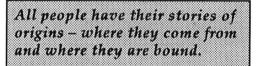

*All people have their stories of origins – where they come from and where they are bound.*

My children, you must understand the role of myth and cosmology. People have myths to explain where others come from, too, and how they stand in relationship to the whole of humankind. The ancient **Greeks,** to the distant north, not only saw themselves at the center of the universe but had a myth to explain how and why Africans are black. They tell us that Phaeton drove his sun chariot too close to the earth and scorched the people of **Ethiopia.**

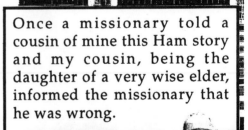

There are others who accept the Biblical curse of Ham – that his son Canaan, and all their descendants will be black – as a sufficient explanation for the color of Africans.

Once a missionary told a cousin of mine this Ham story and my cousin, being the daughter of a very wise elder, informed the missionary that he was wrong.

*All men were originally black. But when Cain killed his brother Abel, and God shouted at him, Cain was so frightened that he turned white and his features shrunk up, making him the first white man.*

From that day forward the missionary never uttered a word from his holy book.

**A**ccording to a creation legend among the **Gikuyu**, when humans began to popu-late the earth, the man Gikuyu was summoned by **Mogai** (the Divider of the Universe) and was given the rivers, the forests, the game – all the gifts of nature.

Meanwhile, Mogai, in all his power and omnipotence, made a big mountain called *Kere-Nyaga* or **Mount Kenya.**

t the summit of this great mountain he carved a resting
lace. It was from the crest that Mogai showed Gikuyu
he full majesty of the land he had bestowed upon him.

He then commanded him to descend and make his home at the center of a cluster of fig-trees (*mikoyo*). Mogai told him that if ever he was in need of anything he should make a sacrifice and raise his hands towards Kere-Nyaga and his request would be granted by the Lord of Nature.

When Gikuyu reached the appointed place amid the fig trees he found a wife, Noombi, waiting for him. How delighted Gikuyu was to find yet another beautiful gift from Mogai.

From their union came several daughters. After the ninth girl, Gikuyu wondered if he would ever have a son, so once more he called upon Mogai.

Gikuyu was told to be patient. He was instructed to go and kill one lamb and one kid and place them under a fig tree near his homestead.

Pour the blood and fat of the two animals on the trunk of the tree. Then you and your family make a big fire under the tree and burn the meat as a sacrifice to me.

When Gikuyu and his family completed the ritual they were told to go home and then return to the sacred tree.

**There they found nine young men who were willing to marry their daughters.**

Gikuyu told the young men he would give his consent only if they promised to live in his homestead under a matriarchal system.

Unable to resist the loveliness of Gikuyu's daughters, the young men agreed to the terms and the weddings were soon held. It is from these marriages, my children, that the Gikuyu of Kenya formed the **original nine clans**.

Before I go on, let me play for you a tune on the **mbira**. The prongs symbolize the several clans of my village. Played in perfect harmony, the music exemplifies the goodwill and peace that prevails there during the harvest season.

I should explain that the women of the Gikuyu were physically stronger and better fighters than the men. They also practised *polyandry* (the custom of having more than one husband). Eventually, they were over-thrown by men who took advantage of the leaders' vulnerability while pregnant. Following this triumph, the men took over the leadership of the community and became heads of the family, thus replacing matriarchal rule with *patriarchy*. They also established the rule of *polygamy* (having more than one wife). It is from such a myth that Lewis Henry Morgan, Karl Marx, Friedrich Engels, and other future thinkers will get their ideas about the nature of ancient societies and how women lost their "mother-right."

21

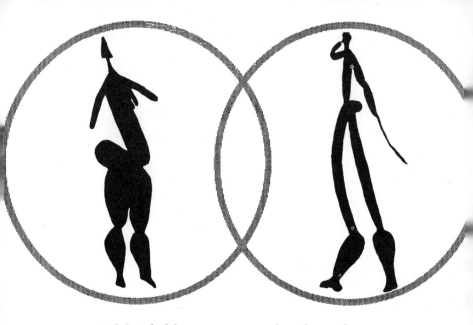

My children, we must be clear about
the differences between *matriarchal*
and *matrilineal*. Matriarchal means
that women rule the society; however,
when a society is matrilineal, it traces
the line of descent through the
females of the family. In my travels I
have seen all sorts of formations, but
most commonly there is a tendency
for the patrilineal (descent through
the father) and the matrilineal to co-
exist in a clan.

There is no conflict. One line of descent usually carries the "blood," while the other carries the "soul," as it is among the **Ashanti.** Among the **Wolof** and the **Baganda**, descent is patrilineal, except for nobility and royalty, who derive from the mother. None of these lines of descent interferes though with the vitality of the extended family, which is the lifeblood of African culture.

To speak as I have of Gikuyu women losing their power to the men brings to mind the story of how the division of labor is maintained among most African villages.

*I*n Gola society, as it is here, the women tend the farms, gather the nuts and berries, and raise the children. It is the duty of the men to hunt and to bring in the meat for the family. However, the griots tell of a man and a woman—a small baby strapped to her back—who were travelling through the bush country when they became very hungry. In a clearing they spotted a herd of cows.

The man, feeling lazy and not much like hunting, said to the woman:

*Since you have the power to change yourself into whatever you desire, change into a leopard and capture one of those grazing cows, so that I can eat.*

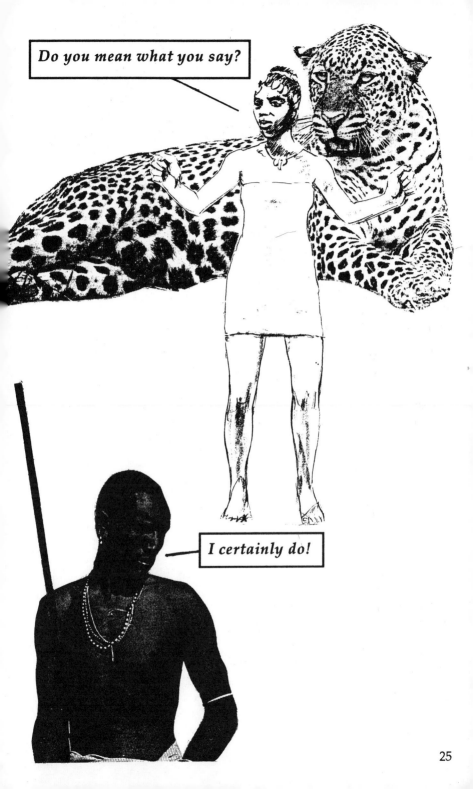

In a matter of moments
the woman had safely
set aside her child and
began transforming
into a leopard.
Spotted hair sprung up
all over her body,
fangs jutted from her
mouth, and her hands
and feet turned into
fierce looking claws.

The man was so terrified
by the transformation that
he hurriedly climbed a tree
for safety. With the man
shaking like a leaf at the
top of the tree, the leopard
ran off to capture a cow.

# JUST KIDDING!

She returned promptly dragging a large cow. Still frightened by all that had transpired, the man begged the leopard to change back into a woman.

Like magic, the leopard's spots began to vanish, the claws retracted and disappeared, and once again the woman was standing below him. But he was still not convinced.

*I will come down only after you have your clothes on and have tied the baby to your back.*

When she had dressed and secured her baby on her back once again, she turned to the man and said:

*Never ask a woman to do a man's work again.*

In some villages it is strictly taboo for a man to touch the tools of a woman. Among the **Dogon**, men carry out the harvesting, while the women gather the stalks and pound the millet. Among the **Shona**, boys, at a very early age, begin to herd cattle and to learn the ways of men, while the girls, by the time they are six, are ready to accompany their mothers to the fields to weed.

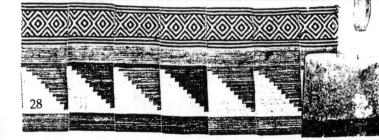

Some of the practices I have seen, though, defy convention, like the nomadic **Wodaabe** of the Sahara. Wodaabe men, who average between 6 and 7 feet tall, participate in a ritual where they adorn themselves with beads and hats, and dye their lips blue to attract a female. During the ceremony, they stand shoulder to shoulder facing the women. To demonstrate their beauty they grimace in such a way as to highlight the whiteness of their teeth and eyeballs.

When a man is chosen by a woman for his beauty, he must spend at least one night with her and if she is pleased, he may receive a marriage proposal.

But the Wodaabe are not alone in finding a unique way to sustain and multiply their clan. The **Lele,** who live along the Kasai River, take no chances. Girls are often betrothed as soon as they are born. Their much older future husbands have to wait until they grow up. In the meantime, the future in-law is expected to do whatever chores the girl's father requests.

By this era, my people, the **Bambara** had domesticated their animals, were cultivating plants, and had begun threshing grain and making flour. The **Stone Age** was a significant transitional period and is an important story told by all the noted griots of the region.

Our culture today has not changed much since those remote times. We are very much like the settled pre-dynastic Egyptians. We hunt and fish, cultivate grain, and make our own clothes and baskets.

30

**Langston Hughes,** a great poet of your time has provided a most fitting preface to this glorious **African Dawn:**

I've known rivers:
I've known rivers ancient as the world
and older than the flow of human blood in
human veins.
My soul has grown deep
like the rivers.
I bathed in the Euphrates when dawns
were young.
I built my hut near the Congo and it lulled
me to sleep.
I looked upon the Nile and raised the
Pyramids above it...
My Soul has grown deep like the rivers.

In our next meeting by Ogun's fire I will tell you about the marvellous civilizations from which we all descend, about **Nubia** and **Kush**; for it is from **Napata** and **Meroe** that the earliest glimmer of refinement and technology first emerged. From these vistas, my children, it is only a short journey up the Nile to the seminal grandeur of **Egypt.**

## Part II

PEOPLE of the NILE

The first vapor of humanity and civilization emerged from the highlands of Central Africa where the Nile splits into several tributaries and virtually disappears into thin air.

Centuries before my ancestors embarked on their odyssey up the Nile, they established kingdoms beyond the sixth cataract in the Sudan, in the Nubian desert and across the rugged terrain of Ethiopia.

They were primarily hunters and fishermen, but they were also skilled in the arts and crafts, and knew and heeded the omens of soothsayers.

A 19th century English griot with a pen and renown Egyptologist, **Sir E.A. Wallis Budge**, in his book *Egypt*, suggests that the builders of these kingdoms may have originated even farther south in **Uganda** and **Punt** or **Somalia**. His words are not untrue, for even before the first pharaoh, this tale was told.

**Kush** and **Nubia** were the most prominent of the predynastic kingdoms that flourished in the Nile Valley. Very little is known of the origins of Kush and much of that is shrouded in legend and myth.

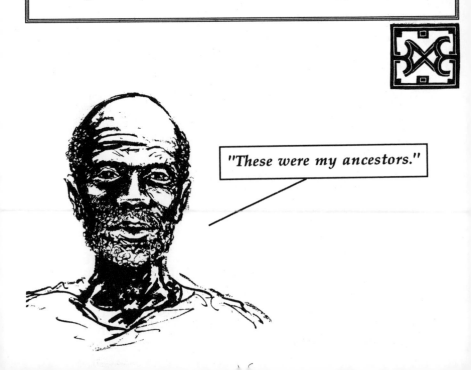

On the other hand, the history of Nubia is well-documented and known to anyone who cares to inquire. It was from this thriving settlement that—having mastered fire, fashioned tools and smelted iron—that Nubians ventured up the Nile before the reign of Menes, 3200 BCE (Before the Christian Era), to influence the culture of Upper Egypt.

*"These were my ancestors."*

This mixed population
of **Tasians**, **Badarians**,
and **Amratians**

cultivated crops

made pottery and axes

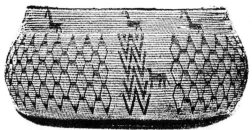

wove baskets

and used instruments
made of flint, copper,
gold, and ivory.

These people, my ancestors, bore the knowledge and
technology that formed, in the words of the honored
Senegalese scholar **Cheikh Anta Diop,** *"the basis of
Egyptian Civilization."*

It would take a team of griots to properly assess the impact of ancient Egyptian culture on the world, but I will do my best to recall its majesty and its seminal role in the sciences, literature, philosophy and technology upon which rest the hallmarks of Greek and Roman civilization.

While many of us know of the importance given to the thought and wisdom of **Socrates, Plato** and **Aristotle**, we know nothing of **Hermes Trismegistus**, the Egyptian founder of wisdom and the sciences, or of **Ptolemy,** the Alexandrian astronomer.

One need only gaze for a moment upon the majesty of the great pyramids or the sphinx at **Giza** to understand how Egyptian scholarship is at the base of Western culture.

*How is it possible to talk about the "glory of Greece and the grandeur of Rome" without understanding the mysteries of Egypt?*

Over the years, being a griot who can see beyond the veil into the future, let me say that it was the unbridled ethnocentrism of European scholars and writers that made it difficult for them to acknowledge the **African character** of Egyptian culture.

When they did recognize the acomplishments of Egypt, they appropriated the culture without accepting its progenitors.

*That, my children, is to have the calabash yet foresake its seed.*

To their thinking, we must assume, if the Egyptians were so remarkable, they must have been Europeans. Even such a celebrated historian as **Arnold Toynbee** in his *Study of History* regarded Egyptian civilization as "white" or European.

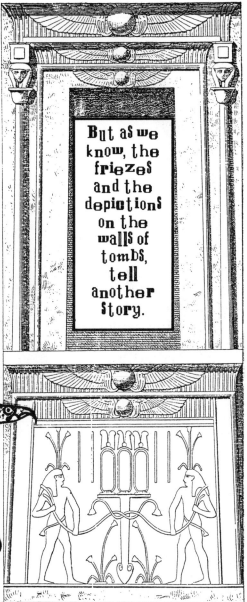

But as we know, the friezes and the depictions on the walls of tombs, tell another story.

These impressive murals indicate that the Egyptians, including the regal queens **Cleopatra** and **Nefertari**, were a dark-skinned people. They certainly could not be mistaken for white in any future land in the West.

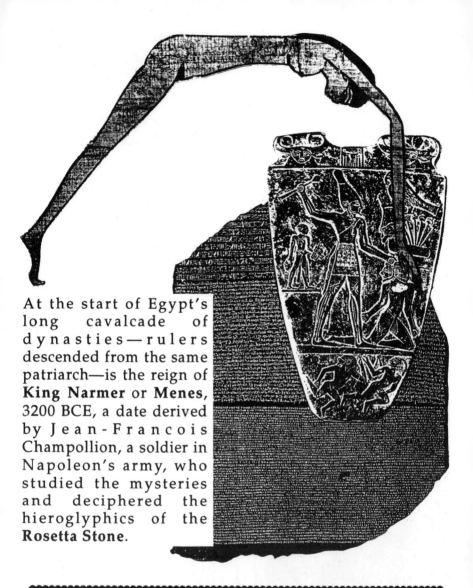

At the start of Egypt's long cavalcade of dynasties—rulers descended from the same patriarch—is the reign of **King Narmer** or **Menes**, 3200 BCE, a date derived by Jean-Francois Champollion, a soldier in Napoleon's army, who studied the mysteries and deciphered the hieroglyphics of the **Rosetta Stone**.

**Menes** was the first pharaoh to unify the **Nile Valley** from Upper to Lower Egypt. It is important to know that when I speak of *Upper and Lower Egypt*, it is done in relation to the Nile River, which flows to the north and empties into the Mediterranean Sea. Lower Egypt is thus in the north and Upper Egypt is in the south. The Nile, like the **Baobab tree** which seems to grow upside down, defies the conventions of nature.

As Pharaoh, Menes was god incarnate, possessing divine attributes, and according to tradition, was placed at the summit of Egyptian society. The resourceful Menes is also credited with founding the **Bull Cult of Apis** at Memphis. There is an indisputable correlation between this cult and the legendary figure of **Minos**, the first king and lawgiver of Crete.

Menes, as with succeeding pharaohs, deemed himself an incarnation of **Horus**, after the royal and national god of Egypt. According to myth, Horus had sovereignty over the whole of Egypt. His rival and brother, **Seth**, had dominion over Upper Egypt. In their struggle for land, the two brothers dismembered each other. Menes's unification of Egypt apparently also brought peace to this myth.

As glorious as the early dynasties of the Old Kingdom were, it was not until the Fourth Dynasty (3766-3633 BCE) some 800 years after the Egyptians invented the calendar (4241BCE) that the age of pyramids gained prominence. Though such towering monuments were indispensable to the cult of the pharaoh, one cannot ignore the tremendous amount of forced labor over generations that was involved in completing those structures.

Mycerinus Chephren Cheop

To erect a shrine befitting the austerity of the pharaoh, thousands of commoners were enslaved for life, and many, to secure the secrets of construction, were entombed with the pharaoh . . . .

Herodotus, the Greek historian who travelled widely, reports that it took 100,000 men 20 years to complete the task.

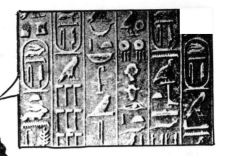

The most imposing of the pyramids built was at **Giza.** Despite being one of the earliest structures of the world, Giza (450 feet tall) contains more stone than any building ever erected, more stone than the fabled walls of Zimbabwe.

Rivalling the pyramids in splendor is the nearby *sphinx*, with its lion's body and human head. Carved entirely in native rock, the sphinx was placed at the entrance to the tombs to guard the Pharaohs.

*Sometimes these sphinxes were ram-headed, signifying wisdom, mystery, and power.*

From the seventh to the 18th dynasty, from the Old Kingdom to the New Kingdom, Egypt experienced phenomenal change and development. During these eventful years a number of things we take for granted today were introduced: the art of **shaving**; the donning of such apparel as **tunics, sandals, kilts**; the wearing of **amulets, wigs, perfumed oils,** and **makeup**; the use of **dyes**; and the invention of **board games** and **musical instruments**. It was also a period of great literary activity, when **poetry, fables,** and **legal writings** were widely disseminated.

This was also a time of social revolution, when royal power was seriously weakened and Egypt was subjugated by Asiatic invaders. But by the reign of **Tutankhamen,** in the 18th Dynasty(1354-1345 BCE), this epoch of national eclipse gave way to Egypt's greatest period of imperial expansion. A parallel development to Egypt's expansion was an internal crisis that virtually halted the kingdom's prosperity for several decades. This crisis arose from the religious reforms enacted by **Akhenaton** or **Amenhotep IV** (1378-54 BCE)

Challenging the Theban priesthood and their god **Amon**, Akhenaton revived the ancient cult of the sun, giving it practical expression in the worship of Aton. All other gods and their temples were repudiated and Akhenaton demanded exclusive worship of Aton.

Many scholars and griots conclude that this religious innovation influenced **monotheism**, one-god systems of belief, that were soon prevalent throughout the fertile crescent. Our own system of belief here in Belandougou harkens back to this genesis.

Despite the resistance from the priesthood and laity, Akhenaton's fervor for Aton was undeniable and is best expressed in this stanza from one of his hymns:

*The fish in the river dart before thy face,*
*and thy rays are in the midst of the great green sea...*
*Thou art in my heart*
*and none knows thee as does thy son,*
*Akhenaton,*
*Whom thou hast made wise with thy designs*
*and thy strength.*

The devotion of Akhenaton and his wife **Queen Nefertiti** to Aton did not suvive the heretic king and within a few years after his death his attempted reform was but a memory.

Under the pressure of the priests, his successor, **Tutankhamen** – the "boy king" – restored Amon and moved the court back to Thebes.

Then, as griot **DuBois** notes in his classic study, came the reigns of **Rameses** I and II:

*"who built monuments all over Egypt and Nubia and fought against the Libyans, Syrians and Hittites."*

This period coincided with the rise of the Hebrew nation in 2500 BCE.

* *Ramses*

With the ascendance of **Rameses III**, decadence was widespread in Egypt, signalling a steady decline in the kingdom. Taking advantage of the social dissolution and political chaos, the Ethiopian kings assumed their control over Egypt's last dynasties, beginning in the 25th Dynasty (712 BCE) under **Piankhi**. As the noted Africanist and 20th century griot **Dr. Yosef A.A. Ben-Jochannan** relates in his book *Black Man of the Nile*:

*"...of the solely indigenous African Pharanic dynasties Piankhi's was one of the most powerful in Egyptian history,"*

Such was the state of things when **Alexander the Great** arrived to add Egypt to his conquests.

At this juncture, let me say that the histories of Egypt and Ethiopia converge with each greatly profitting from the other.

A fabulous legend is told of Alexander's encounter with **Candace, Queen of Meroe**. It is said that she would not allow him to enter Ethiopia and warned him not to deride her people because they were black, asserting that they were "whiter" in soul than his white folk.

She ruled eighty tribes, who were ready to punish those who attacked her.

In many ways, Candace's rule was almost as remarkable as the better known episodes of another Ethiopian Queen— **Sheba**.

According to legend, Queen Sheba ventured to Jerusalem to seek out the wisdom of Solomon. To test Solomon's wisdom, Sheba asked the King of the Jews a series of riddles. This is one example from Jewish legends:

**SHEBA:**

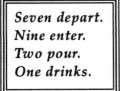

*Seven depart.*
*Nine enter.*
*Two pour.*
*One drinks.*

**SOLOMON:**

*Seven days represents the period of a woman's menstruation; nine months the period of her pregnancy; two pouring is in reference to her breasts; and one drinking, a reference to her baby.*

After an exchange of challenges, Sheba consented to marriage with Solomon, from which union sprang **Prince Menelik,** the Lion of Judah and the forebear of **Emperor Haile Selassie.**

For several centuries the Ethiopian kings warred with the **Assyrians** and the **Persians** for dominance in the Nile Valley. During the Ptolemaic and Hellenistic period (330-30 BC), Egypt was ruled by a succession of Greek monarchs and descendants of **Ptolemy**, including his beautiful, tawny daughter **Cleopatra**.

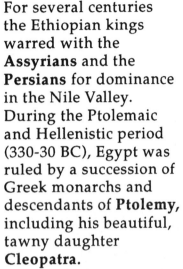

After Cleopatra's death in 30 BC, Egypt was incorporated into the **Roman Empire**. For seven hundred years the Egyptian civilization was overwhelmed by the Romans.

About the same time that **Ergamenes** (1st century BCE) was uniting the so-called nine nations of Ethiopia, the **Punic War** between Europe and Africa was raging on the Western Front. At the onset of the second Punic war, the citizens of the North African city of **Carthage**, led by the brilliant **Hannibal** (247-183 BCE), invaded Spain.

Guiding his army, some riding war elephants, over the treacherous Alps, Hannibal then advanced against **Italy**.

For 13 years the Carthaginians dominated the Italian peninsula, establishing strongholds in **Naples** and **Sicily**. It was only after **Cato the Elder** formed a pact with the rebel **Masinissa** in 146 BCE that the Romans were able to subdue the Carthaginians. Under Roman rule Carthage, which was always rich in textiles, pottery and glassware, became a major supplier of **grains** and **olives** to the Empire.

O nce upon a time, sometime during the period between 332 BCE and the birth of Christ, there arose the highly developed kingdom of **Ghana**. If the date of Ghana's origin is uncertain, its influence on West African history is not, particularly by 700 of the Common Era (CE) when the resourceful **Soninke** people consolidated the territory.

Situated in the northern portion of West Africa, ancient Ghana, despite its extensive boundaries, was hundreds of miles from the region of modern Ghana, *the Gold Coast*. It was strategically located between present day Ghana and the enormous salt deposits to the north in the **Sahara Desert**. Such a position was ideal for exploiting the caravans laden with goods that traversed the territory.

By the 11th Century, Ghana's greatest leader, **Tenkhamenin**, with a well-paid standing army of 200,000, had completely

confederated the villages and small kingdoms surrounding Ghana. Tenkhamenin not only subdued the warring factions, he also neutralized the hordes of **Muslims** from **Morocco** and **Mauretania** amassing at his borders.

**Tuareg** and **Berber** merchants from the Saharan frontiers were indispensable to the market places of Ghana, moving such cherished goods as:

pepper,
kola nuts,
maize,
groundnuts,
and
cassava,

increasing Tenkhamenin's power and influence.

56

The people of **Ghana**, like the other people of this region, were basically agricultural, but trading was also a vital part of their economy. In fact, **Kumbi Saleh**, Ghana's capital, was a major commercial center through which passed all the latest developments in science and culture.

Before the end of the 11th Century, the infusion of **Islam** had touched nearly every sector of Ghanaian society. When Tenkhamenin submitted to the **Almoravids**, a fanatical band of warrior Muslims, the assimilation of Islam was complete, gradually overturning the traditional animistic beliefs. Tenkhamenin's defeat, coupled with a series of severe droughts, marked the end of an empire that would leave its imprint on all the succeeding kingdoms, all of which occupied virtually the same enclave.

# MALI...

which was in ascendance by the middle of the 13th Century, followed Ghana as the major civilization in West Africa and, to a large degree, forged its economy as Ghana had done by taxing the gold and salt merchants.

And as Ghana had its Tenkhamenin, Mali had its **Sundiata Keita**, who was victorious over the Sosso people and sacked Kumbi Saleh.

It is from one of my esteemed descendants, **Mamadou Kouyate**, that you may learn of Sundiata's conquests and how he rose to power.

"Sundiata was immovable," Mamadou says, "so the orders were given and the war drums began to beat. On his proud horse Sundiata turned to the right and to the left in front of his troops...

Having drawn his sword, Sundiata led the charge, shouting his war cry. The Sossos were surprised by this sudden attack for they all thought the battle would be joined the next day. The lightning that flashes across the sky is slower, the thunderbolts less frightening and floodwaters less surprising than Sundiata swooping down on Sosso Balla and his smiths. In a trice, Sundiata was in the middle of the Sossos like a lion in the sheepfold. The Sossos, trampled under the hooves of his fiery charger, cried out. When he turned to the right, the smiths of Soumaoro fell in their tens, and when he turned to the left his sword made heads fall as when someone shakes a tree of ripe fruit.

The horsemen of Mema wrought a frightful slaughter and their long lances pierced flesh like a knife sunk into a paw-paw.

Charging ever forward, Sundiata looked for Sosso Balla; he caught sight of him and like a lion bounded towards the son of Soumaoro, his sword held aloft.

His arm came sweeping down but at that moment a Sosso warrior came between them and was sliced like a calabash. Sosso Balla did not wait and disappeared from amidst his smiths. Seeing their chief in flight, the Sossos gave way and fell into a terrible rout."

It is true that we owe the first days of Mali's ascendance to Sundiata, but the kingdom's most glorious period occurred between 1307 and 1332 under the reign of **Mansa Musa.**

A descendant of the Keita dynasty, Mansa Musa was an astute leader and he tactfully encouraged the industry of his people, urging them to combine agricultural endeavors with crafts and mining.

He was also an ardent Muslim and to fulfill one of the tenets of a devout follower, he organized a massive pilgrimage to **Mecca** in 1324. Included in his large entourage were hundreds of servants, thousands of soldiers and eighty camels bearing twenty-four thousand pounds of gold(most of which he gave away to strangers).

*Not since the grandeur of Egypt or Sheba's caravan to Jerusalem had there been such a lavish display of power, wealth and generosity.*

Akili Ni Mali
— Swahili
(Wisdom is Gold)

For a quarter of a century Mali flourished under the guidance of Mansa Musa. His contact with the East was of mutual benefit. His splendid sense of organization that brought about an accord in the region was well in advance of political developments in Europe, which, during the same period, was still several decades from developing its nation states.

In many respects Mali's decline and fall were similar to Ghana's. First Mansa Musa, the charismatic leader, died, then there were periods of devastating droughts that hampered the economy, and then came the internal feuding and the invasions from **Songhay**. And Songhay too, like the preceeding civilizations, would take full advantage of the gold and salt trade.

Out of the ruins of Mali, as a phoenix rises from its ashes, **Songhay** emerged.

**Sonni Ali** led the assault against Mali, and by 1469 his well-drilled soldiers had leveled **Timbuktu** and the capital of **Niani,** wresting control of Mali's main cities. Ali, no great lover of Islam despite his name, ruled with an iron hand until 1492. He was succeeded by **Askia Muhammad,** Songhay's most gifted king.

Like Mansa Musa, Askia Muhammad was a fervent Muslim, and in 1497 he mounted his own version of a munificent pilgrimage to Mecca. His was indeed an awesome caravan of people and material wealth, but it fell short of matching Mansa Musa's retinue and profusion.

Askia Muhammad's most significant contribution was his administrative ability and his reforms in the realm of education. He encouraged the building of thousands of schools and the **University of Sankore** was a lasting monument to his ideals.

The reign of **Askia the Great**, may his memory be always upon our lips, was one of the longest in the history of the West African kingdoms. It lasted until 1529 when he was overthrown by his son.

Internal dissension combined with marauding renegades, especially the Spanish and Moroccans, signalled the end of Songhay.

TOMB OF ASKIA THE GREAT

Following the splendor of **Ghana, Mali** and **Songhay,** there arose other kingdoms farther to the east near **Lake Chad.**

**Kanen-Bornu** was the most important of these small desert kingdoms, existing from 1220 to the 20th Century. In this arid region the **Berber** people were dominant and the mining of copper brought them great prosperity.

There were also significant empires farther south along the coast of **West Africa**, and into the hinterlands. **Oyo, Benin (Dahomey)**—where the legendary Amazons were said to have reigned—and the powerful **Ashanti** nation are but a few of the political units that developed and spread prior to the coming of the Europeans.

You griots from **Benin** know better than I the legends of your past, of how your elders went to the **Oni of Ife**, the keeper of ritual power, and requested a prince to guide them. Thus came **Oranmiyan**, the founder of **Oyo**. Oranmiyan begat Ewera from whom your present Oba is descended.

> *Let me say that I have visited your kingdom and know of its splendor. I have taken in the beauty of the Oba's court, seen the magnificent galleries and the gates upon gates of pleasing vistas. What abundance awaits a traveller from another plain!*

To see thousands of prancing horses, the brigades of slaves carrying ceramic bowls of water and palm wine and grass for the horses is something to behold. And when the court musicians and dancers appear, arrayed in stunning masks of ebony and cowrie shells, a festive air dominates the city and all of Oyo pays homage to the great founder, **Oranmiyan**, and to the supreme spirit, **Shango**. O, what artistic and poetic richness prevail in this city!

I can foretell the coming of a revolution in Zimbabwe.
Mchawi said:
"the valley's terrain, nourished by the soft winds from the Indian Ocean, was a splendid venue, a verdant clime of fever trees and thickets of sage."

I am reminded, my children, of when the griot **Mchawi** regaled us with tales of **Great Zimbabwe** the impressive empire of the **Monomotapa.**

If there was ever a kingdom to rival Oyo, it was Zimbabwe. Located in the valley of the **Mtilikwe River**, not far from present day **Harare**, the central core of Zimbabwe was a mysterious complex of stone temples, covering some 60 acres of land.

During its most prosperous
phase, Zimbabwe was governed
by **Mutota** of the **Shona** people
who, as Mchawi has said,
divined the plans and strategy
for the construction of the temple
walls. These walls, built without
mortar, still stand as a monument
to Mutota's great vision.

The significance of these scattered
ruins is open for speculation, and
many of my fellow griots have
tried to solve the riddle. I too am
not able to unravel the secrets of
Zimbabwe and the intentions of
its soothsayers. Some contend
that Great Zimbabwe, whose
economy was based on gold, came
into existence about 1000 CE and
that it evolved from the Shona
culture. On this we can agree,
but, it is my contention that Great
Zimbabwe was neither founded
by Solomon or Sheba, nor was it
the special genius of Europeans
who erected these towers of
uncemented stone, as proposed
by the **Cecil Rhodes**, the
infamous English Imperialist.

By my mouth, my attentive griots, it is indisputably true that the **Zulu** invasions of the early 19th Century destroyed Great Zimbabwe and ended one of the most prosperous empires in all of southern Africa. Only the vast kingdoms of the **Congo** and **Kitwara** in **East Africa** were comparable to Zimbabwe's extensive size and influence.

Let me pause here, my listeners, for the hour is growing late. I, too, will drink from the **calabash**, for my mouth is as dry as the Sahara. Remember, my children, we are small beside our ancestors, but we have the benefit of all those yesterdays. So we must heed the words of the wise, which, as the **Mande** know, should be sufficient. I stand at the middle of a long tradition of griots and I have travelled from Alexandria to Zululand to learn the ways of my people. I have sat at the feet of griots steeped in the knowledge of history, language, music, science, and culture.

Ogotemelli of the Dogon, having lost his sight but not his vision, revealed the cosmos for me and told me of Africa's origins from a starburst many æons ago. From Bilal, who lived many years among the Berbers of the Sudan, I gathered my knowledge of the East, how the Yao of Mozambique conquered the Nyasas, and how the Kabakas of Uganda sold their slaves and ivory to the Arabs at good prices.

Yes, my children, I have dreamed long in the villages of the great masters and, as I am compelled to speak the truth. there is much that I have sworn to conceal. Do not seek to know that which is unknowable. It is enough to comprehend that which is yours to know. But remember, the fear of god is the beginning of wisdom. I give you my words as they were given to me by my father, Omawale. As Mamadou Keita reminds us, *"Royal griots cannot lie"* and they know how to venture near the eternal spirits without disturbing their rest ... and it is time that we rest.

## Part III

LAND of the DRUM

*But first a generous libation to the forest gods and those who watch over us beyond the shadows.*

The drums you hear, my children, are in honor of the harvest season which has just begun. Always at twilight at this time of the year there is a major feast and celebration and we give thanks to our **orishas**, the gods who inhabit the fields and the clouds.

It is a tradition among my
people to sing and dance
until the first sign of dark.
We then settle around the
compound fire to hear the
**koras**, the **reed flutes**, the
soft wood **marimbas**, and to
listen to the griots as they
commune with the early
night spirits.

That circle of men under the sheltering palm tree are the master drummers. In this choir there are male and female drums and they must be played in a strict ritualistic pattern if they are to succeed in propitiating the gods, to make them stop and settle in a current of soothing sound, in a brace of the healing force.

The tall drum is male,
it takes the lead,
setting the pace of
the rhythm.

It was shaped from the
**baobab tree** that used to
stand near the village
center. It has absorbed
the essence of our days
and nights and with the
right rhythm a conjurer
can bring back the best of
those memories.

When the **dundun** or **talking drum** enters, my children, it is a signal for the drummers on the wide female drums to prepare. Listen, can you hear the changing tones of the dundun? Let me interpret for you:

millet

corn

*O, Shango, we humble ourselves before you, asking your blessings and your forgiveness for our transgressions. Protect us from the evil spirits who dwell in the swamp and keep us safe from the locusts and our enemies to the North.*

*We offer thanks to you for a bountiful harvest that will nurture us through another season; it is to you that we owe such munificence. You are as wise and as resourceful as the palm tree from which we draw the wine to fill our vessels.*

cassava

banana

rice

Like the silky leaves of the palm tree that we use to make our garments, you envelop us with your tender mercy.

Like the fruit of the palm you satisfy our spiritual hunger and fill us with reverence.

You are strong like the palm tree's nut that contains the refreshing milk.

O, god of the palm tree, keep us strong and resourceful like you, may we burn through the night like the palm oil lamp so that we can continue to honor your blessings and your gifts.

yam

sweet potato

Listen, hear how the dundun softens, how it breathes in concert with the people? Now the full choir can begin as the village comes to life.

Chuma, the lead drummer on the female drum, is a powerful player, but he knows how to temper his beat and make it complement the sound of the smaller female drums. His hands are so fast that only the gods can see them when he plays.

His drum is made of ebony and stretched over with camel skin. Those cowrie shells clustered at the center are a receptacle through which the sound of the male drum enters.

There is a certain cross rhythm that represents a mating call; it is the same easy but determined rhythm you can hear in the night, emanating from each home where young lovers dwell. It is said to be a primal rhythm, a fertility rhythm, that is as old as my people's history.

Chuma is the village smith who makes the great metal masks that the night dancers wear. He is also my wife's brother, and, as is customary among my people, has authority over my children. One of my youngest sons, Mungo, by my third wife, Efua, is training with him to be an ironsmith and a sculptor. The figurines of brass, bronze, and terra cotta decorating the chief's home come from his workshop. Mungo is blessed with great talent; the gods have embraced him and surely blessed his hands.

To speak of our origins is to recall the prophecy and lore that has been passed down through the great blind griot **Ogotemelli** the Dogon. For our beginning was much like theirs. As Ogotemelli relates:

*The God Amma...took a lump of clay, squeezed it in his hand and flung it from him, as he had done with the stars. The clay spread and fell on the north, which is the top, and from there stretched out to the south, which is the bottom of the world.*

The earth lies flat...It extends
east and west with separate
members like a fetus in the
womb. This body, lying flat,
face upwards, in a line from
north to south, is feminine.
Its sexual organ is an anthill,
and its clitoris a termite hill.
Amma, being lonely and
desirous of intercourse with
this creature, approached it.
That was the occasion of the
first breach of the order of the
universe.

This creation, according to the long line of griots who preceded Ogotemelli, was Amma's first blunder.

*At the god's approach, the termite hill rose up, barring passage and displaying its masculinity.*

*It was as powerful and potent as the organ of the stranger, and there was no possibility of intercourse.*
*But, as we have learned, Amma was all-powerful. He cut down the termite hill and had intercourse with the excised earth.*

*The twins Amma had expected from the union did not come forth; instead came the jackal.*

Only after water was introduced in the following unions did the twins arrive. These spirits were called Nommo and were of divine essence like Amma.

Later, after the Nommo came down to earth and entered the anthill to protect their mother against the incestuous advance of the jackal, the male aspect of Nommo took the place of the masculine element, while the female Nommo took the place of the female element, and her womb became part of the womb of the earth.

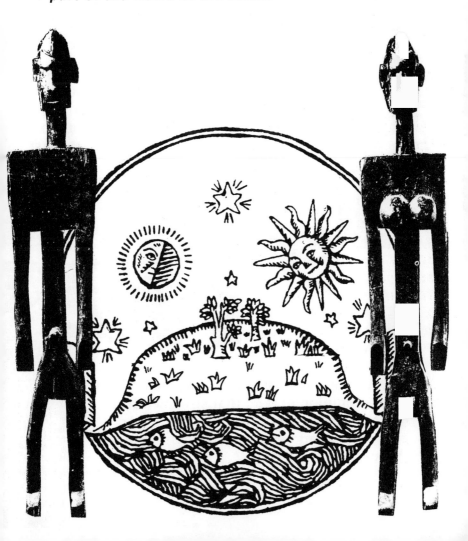

*Earlier, if you recall, I remarked of the splendors of Timbuktu, did I not?*

But now the changing pattern of the drums says that it is time to speak again of great leaders and the cultures I have known in my travels across the length and breadth of the continent.

I should tell you now of my stay in Timbuktu with a descendant of **Ahmed Baba,** the last chancellor of the **University of Sankore.**

He was a wealthy man who presided over a large dominion of land that stretched from one horizon to the other. All of this land and wealth had been passed down to him through the Baba clan.

Ahmed Baba was a brilliant man and authored more than forty books in his lifetime; each book discussed, at great length, a different topic.

It was his misfortune to be in Timbuktu when it was invaded by the Moroccan hordes near the end of the 16th Century.

Ahmed Baba was courageous before the invaders, never giving any ground. Eventually, it has been written, Ahmed Baba was imprisoned and sent to Morocco. Meanwhile, his enormous library of more than 1500 books, so cherished by scholars near and far, was lost forever. That is, all but a precious few, which were maintained by the family and hidden away from thieves, and for posterity.

The legend of these books and their whereabouts is much like the myth that surrounds **Prester John**, the African Christian king who was the quest of Portuguese pirates and conquistadors as early as the 15th Century. Many speak of them, but the evidence remains a mystery.

My generous host at Timbuktu plied me with many stories and many gifts before I had to travel on to **Bushongoland**.

.Timbuktu

CONGO

> *Kill neither man, woman, nor child. Are they not the children of Chembe, and have they not the right to live?*

Perhaps you have heard your elders speak of the great kings of the **Congo**. Let me tell you about **Shamba Bolongongo**, who ruled with firmness and serenity. He was the son of a **Manikongo** and thus inherited his rule. He is best recalled as a ruler who prohibited the use of the **shongo**, a throwing knife which is the traditional weapon of the Bushongo.

It was his belief that we should "kill neither man, woman, nor child. Are they not the children of Chembe (God), and have they not the right to live?" I hope it is remembered that Shamba reigned during the Congo's "Golden Age," when warfare was virtually abolished, when raffia weaving and the other peaceful arts were introduced.

Pottery, as you may recall, is the first attested invention of God.

Hold a true friend with both thy hands.

— Kanuri

This was a period when **pottery** was molded from village to village, when the technique of weaving (which is like making a drum) was done in nearly every family, and sculpture was created in great profusion all over Africa.

**Weaving**, the interlacing of warp and weft, the clapping of the shuttle and the creaking of the block, makes way for the Word.

Even here in our village you can see aspects of the Bushongo's prowess.

*Look!*

This wooden cup, carved in the form of a human head with the curled horns of a ram, I brought back from the **Congo**. It is used only for drinking the ritual **palm wine**.

This mask, too, is from Bushongo. Observe how the beadwork follows the median line of the nose and mouth and along the eyebrows. As you can see, those are cowrie shells that ornament the top.

You ask of the figure there studded with nails, knives and other pieces of iron? That is called **Konde**. It was given to me by a **Bakongo** merchant.

In fact, there are many artifacts here in the village from Bakongo. Many of the Bakongo fled here after the terrible wars with the **Portuguese**.

After several years of fierce battles, the Manikongos were defeated by the Portuguese invaders and their kingdoms fell into disarray. The griots who live at the far end of the village can relate their history much better than I.

That wooden harp of which you inquire comes from my days with the **Mangbetu,** who live at the edge of the **Ituri Rainforest**. The Mangbetu are known for their habit of binding their children's heads to elongate them in a graceful fashion. The woman's head at the top of the harp is exemplary of this practice.

I will tell of only one more
piece of art, for the night
drums are settling down to
a whisper and the time will
soon come when we must
preserve the sacred silence.

100

That headdress with the hollow hemispherical base was passed on to me by one of my elders many years ago.

It is a ceremonial headdress from the **Egungun** society and is used in its plays in honor of the ancestors. The Egungun are a cult of the **Yoruba** who number many millions.

The **Yoruba** of ancient **Ife**, I should relate, were also gifted artists. They founded a school of naturalistic bronze and terra cotta sculpture that is unsurpassed in all of Africa, if not in the lands beyond the seas.

It was my privilege to be in Yorubaland during the funeral of **King Oyo** and to witness a glorious display of artwork.

The King was buried in a bara, which was surrounded by all kinds of bronze and terra cotta figurines. It was at night, but you could see the figures glistening in the moonlight.

The ceremony began with a blare from an ivory trumpet and the sound of a koso drum, much like the one Chuma is beating. This drum is normally beaten every morning at four as a signal for the king to arise. Thus to beat it at night indicated that he was retiring to his final resting place.

Unlike the customs of my people, the king was buried with lavish gifts made of bronze and terra cotta. And some of his favorite slaves committed suicide in order to serve him in the other world.

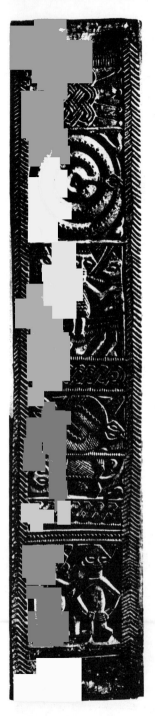

It would be a grave injustice and a possible desecration to speak of the Yoruba and not mention their many gods.

Among the pantheon of over 200 deities that populate the Yoruba spirit world are:

**Eshu**,

spirit of

individuality

and change

# Ifa,

## god

## of

## divination

# Ogun,

### lord

### of

### iron

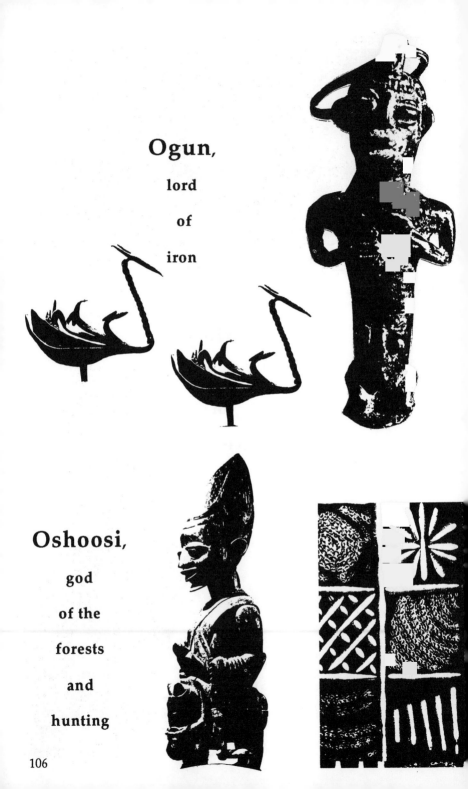

# Oshoosi,

### god

### of the

### forests

### and

### hunting

# Obaluaiye,

### dread spirit of disease and earth;

## The mighty

# Shango,

### fiery

### thunder

### god.

This staff in the form of a kneeling female figure with symbolic thunderbolts on top of her head comes from the cult of **Shango** and is used by dancers seeking to become possessed. It conveys the idea of female service to the god, whose temples are always in the charge of priestesses.

Shango's presence is manifested in this poem of flashing images:

Water by the side of fire at the center of the sky
A strange thing, on the road to Teji Oku
He strikes a stone in the forest, stone bleeds blood
He carries a heavy stone upon his head without cushion.
Shango splits the wall with his falling thunderbolt.

He makes a detour in telegraphic wire
Leopard of the flaming eyes
Lord who wears the sawtooth-bordered cloth returning ancestors (egun)
Storm on the edge of a knife.
Earthworm, despite no eyes, plunges deep into the earth
He dances savagely in the courtyard of the impertinent
He sets the liar's roof on fire
He carries fire as a burden on his head
The gaze of this leopard sets the roof on fire.

Father, grant us the intelligence to avoid
saying stupid things
Against the unforeseen, let us do things
together.
Swift king, appearing like the evening moon.
His very gaze exalts a person.
I have an assassin for a lover.
Beads of wealth blaze upon his frame.

Who opens wide his eyes
Leopard of the flaming eyes
Fire, friend of hearth.
Leopard, of the copper-flashing eyes
Fire, friend of hearth.
Lord with flashing, metallic eyes,
With which he terrifies all thieves.

I can see that you are weary and ready to rest. I will save for another evening my adventures among the **Lozi**, who live along the **Zambesi**. Yes, I have travelled beyond the great rivers and into the heart of **Shonaland**. I can still hear the children at play, singing their songs:

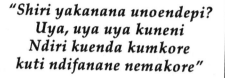

*"Shiri yakanana unoendepi?
Uya, uya uya kuneni
Ndiri kuenda kumkore
kuti ndifanane nemakore"*

(Beautiful bird, where are you off to? Come on, come to me I am going right into the clouds so that I can be part of them.)

I have seen the majestic sunsets on the Mediterranean where ancient **Carthage** loomed and waded in the waters under the shadow of the great **Rock of Gibraltar**. In the maze of **Casablanca**, in the casbah where dancing boys entertained sheiks, I have drunk the mint tea and smoked of the magical hookah. In my seventy harvests, no coast of the continent has escaped my gaze.

I have looked across the Indian Ocean from Kilwa and sailed with friendly Swahili fishermen. I vividly recall their constant chatter:
"Njoo samaki, njoo samaki" (come fish, come fish).

*Njoo samaki, njoo samaki.*

*Njoo samaki, njoo samaki.*

I have seen the miasma sweep over the **Azores** and dust the **Canary Islands**, I have challenged the rough course of the **Congo River** as it crossed the **Equator**, and I have listened in stunned wonder to the deafening roar of the falls at the end of the **Zambesi River**, *Mosi o Tunda*, smoke and thunder, the Shona call it.

I have travelled the long, dangerous road from **Mbeya** to **Kapiri Mposhi**, watched the frolic of wildebeest and rhino on the plains of the **Serengeti**.

I drank blood and milk with the **Maasai**, lived among the **Sotho** on both sides of the Fish River, hunted with the **Khoisan** (the people from the north will call them "bushmen" and "hottentots") of the **Kalahari Desert**.

I have spent many sunsets with the **Mbuti** "pygmy" of the **Ituri Rainforest**. The ingenuity of the Mbuti can be seen in their use of the bow and arrow: it is part weapon, part igniter of fire, and part musical instrument. They live deep in the rainforest where only those daring enough to ride the rapids of the Congo can see them.

Their villages, like the Dogon, are laid out like a mask. At the top are the men's houses and where the iron smith keeps his bellows. The family houses are the eyes of the mask.

The altar at the center of the village is the nose, and below this is a stone for crushing millet that resembles a mouth.

On both sides of the center of the village, like ears, are the houses of the women.

Like the religion of the Mbuti, it took me many nights to understand the significance of this practice, which I have sworn not to relate.

But now, my children, the drums have halted, and only the lilting kora knows the heart of the darkness.  The deep night is upon us and it is time for silence, time to listen to the night spirits, time to rest and prepare for another African dawn . . . and the tongue of Olagun rests.

*To be continued . . .*

# TIME LINE

| | |
|---|---|
| 40,000 BCE | Grimaldi, an early homo sapiens, ventures from Africa |
| 4241 BCE | Invention of a fixed calendar in Egypt |
| 3200 BCE | The reign of King Narmer (or Menes) |
| 3000 BCE | Imhotep, deified as the god of medicine in Egypt |
| 2500 BCE | Rise of the Hebrew nation |
| 1370-1352 BCE | Pharaoh Amenhotep (Akenaton) and Queen Nefertiti introduce Ra, the Sun God |
| ?-1349 BCE | Tutankhamen, or King Tut, rules Egypt |
| 1050 BCE | Queen Sheba travels from Kush to visit Solomon, King of the Jews |
| 712 BCE | Piankhi, an Ethiopian, becomes pharaoh of Egypt |
| 332-283 BCE | Conquest of Egypt by Alexander the Great. Ptolemy, a Macedonian, installed as Pharaoh. |
| 247-183 BCE | Hannibal rules Carthage and invades Italy |
| 47-30 BCE | Cleopatra VIII, Queen of the Nile, rules Egypt |

| | |
|---|---|
| 1-33 CE | Life and times of Jesus Christ |
| 189-199 CE | Pope Victor I, an African, unifies Catholic Church |
| 622 CE | Prophet Muhammed journeys from Mecca to Medina |
| 700-1,076 CE | Ancient empire of Ghana rises under the leadership of Tenkhamenin |
| 1100 CE | Great Zimbabwe flourishes under Monomotapa |
| 1230-1255 CE | Sundiata comes to power in Mali |
| 1324 CE | Mansa Musa of Mali makes pilgrimage to Mecca |
| 1490 CE | Askia Muhammad founds University of Sankore at Timbuktu |
| 1506 CE | King Alfonso of the Kongo ascends to the throne |
| 1590 CE | Songhay empire destroyed by Moroccans |
| 1630 CE | Queen Nzinga organizes the state of Matamba |
| 1650 CE | Great kingdom of Oyo reaches its peak in West Africa |
| 1695 CE | Osei Tutu founds the Ashanti Nation |

# Bibliography

Balandier, Georges, and Jacques Maquet, eds., *Dictionary of Black African Civilization*, Leon Amiel, New York, 1974.

Ben-Jochannan, Yosef A.A., *Africa: Mother of Western Civilization*, Black Classic Press, Baltimore, 1988.

————, *Black Man of the Nile and His Family*, Black Classic Press, 1989.

Bernal, Martin, *Black Athena*, Rutgers University Press, New Jersey, 1987.

Brain, Robert, *Art and Society in Africa*, Longman, London, 1980.

Budge, E.A. Wallis, *Egyptian Language*, Dover Publications, New York, 1983.

Cottrell, Leonard, *Lady of the Two Lands—Five Queens of Ancient Egypt*, Bobbs-Merrill, New York, 1967.

Davidson, Basil, *African Kingdoms, Time-Life Books*, New York, 1966.

————, *Discovering Our African Heritage*, Ginn and Company, Boston, 1971.

Dent, Anthony, *African Rock Art*, Clarkson N. Potter, New York, 1965.

Drewal, Henry John, *Traditional Art of the Nigerian Peoples*, Museum of African Art, Washington, DC, 1977.

Du Bois, W.E.B., *The World and Africa*, International Publishers, New York, 1972.

Elisofon, Eliot, *The Nile*, Viking Press, New York, 1964.

Ezra, Kate, *Art of the Dogon*, Metropolitan Museum of Art, New York, 1988.

Farsi, S.S., *Swahili Sayings from Zanzibar*, Kenya Literature Bureau, Nairobi, 1958.

Franklin, John Hope, *From Slavery to Freedom*, Alfred Knopf, New York, 1980.

Griaule, Marcel, *Conversations with Ogotemmêli: An Introduction to Dogon Religious Ideas*, Oxford University Press, London, 1965.

Harris, Joseph E., *Africans and Their History*, New American Library, New York, 1978.

Jackson, John G., Introduction to African Civilizations, Citadel Press, New York, 1970.

Jaritz, Horst, *Nubians in Egypt*, University of Texas Press, Austin, 1973.

Kenyatta, Jomo, *Facing Mount Kenya*, London, 1938.

Leakey, Richard, and Roger Lewin, *Origins*, E.P. Dutton, New York, 1977.

Mair, Lucy, African Societies, *Cambridge University Press*, London, 1974.

Mazrui, Ali A., *The Africans—A Triple Heritage*, BBC Publications, London, 1986.

Monti, Nicholas, ed., *Africa Then*, Alfred Knopf, New York, 1987.

Motley, Mary Penick, *Africa: Its Empires, Nations and People*, Wayne State University Press, Detroit, 1969.

Murray, Jocelyn, ed., *Cultural Atlas of Africa*, Facts on File Publications, New York, 1982.

Niane, D.T., *Sundiata: An Epic of Old Mali*, Longman, Essex, England, 1960.

Oliver, Roland, and Caroline Oliver, eds., *Africa in the Days of Exploration*, Prentice Hall, New Jersey, 1965.

Oliver, Roland, and J.D. Fage, *A Short History of Africa*, Penguin, Middlesex, England, 1962.

Parrinder, Geoffrey, *African Mythology*, Paul Hamlyn, London, 1967.

Patrick, Richard, *Egyptian Mythology*, Octopus Books, London, 1972.

Plass, Margaret, *African Tribal Culture*, University Museum, Philadelphia, 1956.

Reck, David, *Music of the Whole Earth*, Charles Scribner's Sons, New York, 1977.

Segy, Ladislas, *Masks of Black Africa*, Dover Publications, New York, 1976.

Sertima, Ivan Van, ed., *Great African Thinkers (Cheikh Anta Diop)*,Transaction Books, New Jersey, 1987.

Thompson, Robert Farriss, *Flash of the Spirit*, Vintage Books, New York, 1984.

West, John Anthony, *Serpent in the Sky—The High Wisdom of Ancient Egypt*, Julian Press, New York, 1979.

Willett, Frank, African Art, *Thames and Hudson*, London, 1970.

Williams, Geoffrey, *African Designs from Traditional Sources*, Dover Publications, New York, 1971.

Williams, John A., *Africa: Her History, Lands and People*, Cooper Square Publications, New York, 1962.

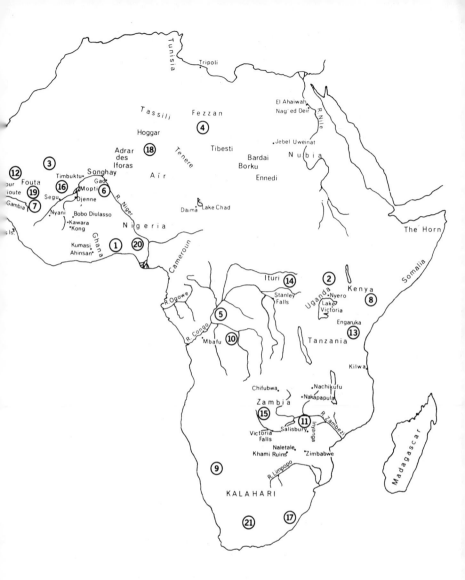

1. Ashanti
2. Baganda
3. Bambara
4. Berbers
5. Congo
6. Dogon
7. Fulani
8. Gikuyu
9. Kadisan
10. Lele
11. Lozi
12. Mandingo
13. Masai
14. Mbuti
15. Shona
16. Soninke
17. Sotho
18. Wodaabe
19. Wolof
20. Yoruba
21. Zulu

**Herb Boyd,** like Olagun, has traveled extensively in Africa. His first book, *The Former Portuguese Colonies in Africa,* was published by Franklin Watts.

Such a project as this — assembled from hundreds of books and shaped by the words of countless informants — owes its creation to many friends and scholars. Most immediate is Shey (you brought the words to life), Glenn (without you African Dawn would have never broken), Marie (who set the stage), and Elza (my loving consort, upon whom the whole trip depended). The bibliography offers some idea of the vital resources we used, but there are several griots — Monroe, Malik, John Henrik Clarke — who were indispensable to the completion of this book. Of course, a success has many claimants, but the faults here belong to me alone.

**Shey Wolvek-Pfister** is a painter and illustrator. This is her fourth "For Beginners" book.

Designing and illustrating this glorious book has been a labor of love, sweat and tears. Along the road with me giving invaluable help and support were:
Herb (an inspiring and tireless griot), Glenn (a true man of vision), Aquina (for your talent and good heart), Sam (whose love, patience and support carried me over the bumpy parts), Kate (whose child energy and innocence was the reminder), Mike Hertz (who gave me space and a hard time), Dave Gilden (a magnificent kora player and photographer*), Garden Copy (who worked with me on the reproductions), of course, Sido (who kept the boards warm with his furry body), and, most of all, Knox Martin (who taught me to see).
Thank you all.

* Dave Gilden Photos: PP 7,67,78,79

# BLACK HISTORY
## FOR BEGINNERS

### DENISE DENNIS

One of the most popular Beginners books. Covering a rich history often ignored, Dennis chronicles the struggle from capture and enslavement in Africa right up through civil rights and the different kinds of struggle African Americans face today.

"This excellent little book on black history...is very readable and informative....It faces the issue of black people's omission from history head on."          -- *The Teacher*

# Writers and Readers Beginners Books

African History for Beginners ...............................................8.95 _____
Architecture for Beginners...............................................7.95 _____
Black History for Beginners...............................................7.95 _____
Black Women for Beginners...............................................8.95 _____
The Brain for Beginners ...............................................8.95 _____
Brecht for Beginners ...............................................7.95 _____
Capitalism for Beginners ...............................................6.95 _____
Computers for Beginners ...............................................7.95 _____
Cuba for Beginners ...............................................6.95 _____
Darwin for Beginners...............................................6.95 _____
DNA for Beginners ...............................................6.95 _____
Ecology for Beginners ...............................................6.95 _____
Economists for Beginners ...............................................4.95 _____
Einstein for Beginners ...............................................6.95 _____
Elvis for Beginners ...............................................6.95 _____
Erotica for Beginners...............................................8.95 _____
Food for Beginners...............................................7.95 _____
French Revolution for Beginners...............................................7.95 _____
Freud for Beginners ...............................................6.95 _____
Hemingway for Beginners ...............................................8.95 _____
Ireland for Beginners...............................................6.95 _____
Judaism for Beginners ...............................................7.95 _____
Lenin for Beginners ...............................................6.95 _____
London for Beginners ...............................................6.95 _____
Malcolm X for Beginners ...............................................8.95 _____
Mao for Beginners...............................................6.95 _____
Marx for Beginners...............................................6.95 _____
Marx for Beginners (Second Edition) ...............................................8.95 _____
Marx's *Kapital* for Beginners ...............................................6.95 _____
Media and Communications for Beginners ...............................................8.95 _____
Medicine for Beginners ...............................................4.95 _____
Nicaragua for Beginners ...............................................7.95 _____
Nietzsche for Beginners ...............................................7.95 _____
Nuclear Power for Beginners ...............................................6.95 _____
Orwell for Beginners...............................................4.95 _____
Pan-Africanism for Beginners ...............................................8.95 _____
Peace for Beginners...............................................6.95 _____
Philosophy for Beginners ...............................................8.95 _____
Plato for Beginners...............................................7.95 _____
Psychiatry for Beginners ...............................................6.95 _____
Rainforests for Beginners...............................................8.95 _____
Reagan for Beginners ...............................................4.95 _____
Reich for Beginners...............................................6.95 _____
Sex for Beginners...............................................7.95 _____
Socialism for Beginners ...............................................6.95 _____
Trotsky for Beginners ...............................................6.95 _____
U.S. Constitution for Beginners...............................................7.95 _____
Virginia Woolf for Beginners...............................................7.95 _____
World War II for Beginners...............................................8.95 _____
Zen for Beginners...............................................6.95 _____